Americana Soul

LUKE CALDWELL

Photography by Danica Cusack

AMERICANA SOUL

HOMES DESIGNED WITH LOVE, COMFORT, AND INTENTION

SIMON ELEMENT

NEW YORK   LONDON   TORONTO   SYDNEY   NEW DELHI

SIMON
ELEMENT

An Imprint of Simon & Schuster, Inc.
1230 Avenue of the Americas
New York, NY 10020

First Simon Element hardcover edition October 2022

SIMON ELEMENT is a trademark of Simon & Schuster, Inc.

For information about special discounts for bulk purchases, please contact Simon &
Schuster Special Sales at 1-866-506-1949 or business@simonandschuster.com.

The Simon & Schuster Speakers Bureau can bring authors to your live event.
For more information or to book an event, contact the Simon & Schuster Speakers
Bureau at 1-866-248-3049 or visit our website at www.simonspeakers.com.

Interior design by Matt Ryan
Photography by Danica Cusack

Manufactured in China

10 9 8 7 6 5 4 3 2 1

Library of Congress Cataloging-in-Publication Data has been applied for.

ISBN 978-1-9821-8740-8
ISBN 978-1-9821-8741-5 (ebook)

Miranda, there is no one like you. I love
that we are on this journey in life together,
and I am forever inspired by your consistent
love and intentionality. I love you.

To each of my wonderful kids,
you bring joy and meaning to our lives.

CONT

E N T S

Introduction

I never thought I would be a designer. I am neither technically trained nor formally educated as one. But growing up, I always appreciated all things creative and beautiful and was drawn to one-of-a-kind spaces.

Whenever I'm asked how I launched a career in design, it's always interesting to stop and think about how this whole journey started for me. In 2010, my wife, Miranda, and I wanted to adopt a child, but we couldn't afford to do so. I decided to buy an old, decrepit home and infuse it with life and sell it to pay for the adoption. That led to many more home restorations and, surprisingly, many more adoptions. Not long after that we were approached by HGTV about creating a show on which we could share all the things we'd learned from renovating and designing homes to sell. Looking back, I realize now that design and I were meant to be. Design was going to be a part of my personal story, and I'm thankful to be able to share what I've learned over the years with you.

Most thrilling for me is that I've had the good fortune to work on projects that reflect different cultures and styles. That's what I find so inspiring about my work: I collaborate with many different clients, and each one is unique. The only constant is that everyone's rooms and environments feel most welcoming and timeless when they have *soul*—when they're unique to the owner, when they've been added to and cared for, and when love is incorporated into each decision. Good design is like a favorite pair of jeans: the fit becomes more comfortable over time.

This book is about the importance of infusing soul—life, heirlooms, character, all the things you love, and, ultimately, your story—into every aspect of your home. I chose the title *Americana Soul* because I believe every person living in this country has a powerful and meaningful story to tell. Every person, from New York City to small-town USA, has a story about their culture, their heritage. We all have something to impart, and design is just one place to share our meaningful journey.

I have a personal connection to each home in this book. Some are my places, while others are those that I worked on for family or clients. All the homes are meaningful to me, and I'm excited to tell you their stories and describe what makes each one authentic and unique.

My Design Philosophy

Home is a place to, above all, enjoy moments, gather as a family, and connect with loved ones. Home should be comfortable and casual, a place where anyone who enters will feel loved, accepted, and heard—a place where we all feel connected to ourselves and others.

Intention is the key to good design, and I begin every project with three core objectives: finding the focus, creating the feel, and emphasizing the details. These three components help me create the overall vision as we move through each design. They're touchstones that enable me to remain true to the purpose of each project throughout the process.

Finding the Focus

At the beginning of every project, the first thing I do is ask, "What is the ultimate goal for this space?" The focus of a project is important, because it can be easy to get bogged down in the details and lose sight of the main goal. The focus dictates every decision I make on the flow and the feel, and even down to the finishes that end up going in the space. Everyone has different needs and priorities for their home. Once you determine what your space is going to be used for (to entertain, to rest, to work), it's much easier to understand your focus.

For example, when finding the focus for my own home, I envisioned a beautiful space that was simple and uncluttered. Livability was just as important as aesthetics. Miranda and I have eight children, some of whom have special needs, including a son who uses a wheelchair. So when I designed our home, my focus was clear: to create an environment that accommodated each child and helped them become who they were meant to be. From the functionality of the floor plan to the selection of the finishes, making a space that would work for my family was my goal.

Before putting pencil to paper, it's important to ask yourself, "What is my *why*?" Thoughtfully answering that question will help you define the focus of the space and lay the foundation for all the design decisions you'll make moving forward.

Creating the Feel

Once you've identified your focus, determine how you want your space to feel. This can sound ambiguous, but all design creates a feeling. Good or bad, it's there when you walk into any space. Before I became a designer, I was in a band, and I wrote songs. I discovered that the feel of the song was critical to its success. You can create a mood and a feeling through a combination of melodies, notes, and lyrics, but the pieces have to work harmoniously together to create a cohesive composition. The same is true with design. The feel of the space is influenced by textures, materials, colors, and finishes. Intentional design creates a feeling, such as boldness, peace, or sophistication.

The feel of your space should also communicate your story—what you want to share with someone who visits your home—or the atmosphere that you want to evoke. Everyone gets a feeling when they walk into a specific place, whether it be a restaurant, a bar, or a boutique hotel. Even when you walk into a jazz club in New Orleans, the environment consumes you. You feel the moody color on the walls, the vintage artwork, the romantic lighting, and the ambient music.

So think about your space: Now that you know the focus, how do you want it to feel? What emotions do you want to inspire in people when they walk into your newly designed space? Layering your design decisions will help you realize that feel.

Emphasizing the Details

The third and final step of my design process—figuring out all the details—is my personal favorite. This is where the design comes to life. Once I understand the focus and know what feeling I wish to create, the details allow me to bring those things to fruition. Colors, finishes, hardware, found objects—each and every one of these details will give your space its new identity.

When I designed our home, one of my focuses was to create a place that was beautiful and durable for my large family, while also having an industrial modern feel. I selected aggregate concrete flooring that was practical but also gave a warm, finished look. The details brought the focus and the feel into harmony.

Choosing all the elements that make up the details can be overwhelming. You won't choose them all overnight. But knowing what your focus is and being loyal to the feel you're trying to achieve will help you get there. And, of course, you can always continue to curate and add details to your unique story.

What Is Americana Soul?

To me, soul is an elusive, hard-to-define but essential element that lies at the core of who we are. Soul gives depth and meaning to people, places, and even objects.

A neighborhood lined with hundred-year-old trees has soul. The trees have a story to tell, a beauty that can't be reproduced. It takes years of nurturing and love and decades of life for those trees to grow. I love the idea of what the trees have seen: kids growing up, people moving through their days, family milestones. The *soul* is felt. I think that's why I'm so drawn to vintage pieces and heirlooms. They have a character and uniqueness to them that you can't mass-produce. They tell a story, one that's passed down through generations. That's what soul is: the experiences you've had, the moments you've lived through, the places you've been, and the people with whom you've shared it all. That's all part of your soul, and it should become part of your story within your home.

Americana Soul is about reveling in the history and soul of what truly makes us individuals. We are all on a journey, and part of that journey is discovering who we really are and what we're passionate about. Beautiful design happens when we allow those discoveries to come to life. I hope that this book will speak to you about how to showcase your passion, history, individuality, family, and culture in your home. The one thing I always come back to is the fact that rooms, spaces, and environments always feel more welcoming, cozy, classic, and timeless when they have soul—when they're unique to each owner and incorporate love into every detail, choice, and intention.

Mixing in sentimental pieces like the childhood tackle box centered on the mantel is the perfect way to create unique, livable spaces with deep meaning.

PART I

Timber & LOVE

arly in my design career, I was drawn to the natural elements found in wood and the ways wood was integrated into homes. I especially loved—and still love—hardwood floors and the warmth and character they bring to a space. The older they are, the more I love them. The first house I purchased was a 1930s cottage in Boise's historic North End district, and the warmth and coziness that the hardwood floors brought to the space was one of the things that drew me to it. To this day, after renovating more than one hundred homes, one of the things I most look forward to when I start a project is pulling up old carpeting, seeing wood floors underneath, and knowing that they'll tell a story. The older and more repurposed the wood, the more character it brings to the home.

Wood is special because every piece is different; every grain tells a different story. It's versatile: whether you use it on the interior or the exterior, it brings warmth. Perhaps it's because I'm from Idaho and have always been drawn to old, rustic cabins, but I knew when I started designing that I would always want timber to play a role in my work. There's always a place for it. You'll see that throughout this book.

It might sound cheesy, but I believe that when we're motivated by love in what we're doing in life and in design and in our homes and in our families, beautiful things emerge. I've never wanted to do something just to make money. Rather, I want to be part of a story. I want to enable love to spark, to create that warm, nestled spot where you can connect with your kids on a Sunday morning. It all starts with love. Good design has love in the foreground.

There are, of course, dozens of elements that go into the homes I design, but at the core of my work is a love for the warmth of wood and a love for the people I work with, the homes I design for them, and our ability to create special places for special moments. Those are the spaces that have soul—an Americana Soul where beauty and life and story come together.

Industrial **Modern**

Any time you're designing something from scratch, there's the potential to feel overwhelmed by the process. There are so many different designs, styles, and avenues to choose from, but remember to make choices that work for your specific needs and tastes. Always refer to your project focus and allow the priorities and feel to guide you in making these decisions.

The exterior vision I had for this new build, which ultimately became our home, started with the beautiful sixty-year-old pine trees. I wanted the driveway to wrap around these established trees; that's where I felt the story of the home should begin. I wanted the house to feel tucked back into nature so that when someone approached, they would first experience the presence of this wooded area. I wanted the home to feel integrated into the neighborhood.

It's important to have varied textural elements in design. Here, I incorporated wood into the entrance, the garage door, and the trim, but used it in three different ways. The contrast between the wood and the black paint and industrial metal features makes the entrance striking. And the consistent use of wood ties everything together so that it feels cohesive.

One thing I've learned is that you can never go wrong with glass. I'm a firm believer in natural light; the more

The fireplace is the focal point of the room. Overscale, it makes a statement. It's framed in a custom-designed, powder-coated sheet metal that makes it feel even larger.

The exterior vision I had for this new build, which ultimately became our home, started with the beautiful sixty-year-old pine trees. I wanted the driveway to wrap around these established trees; that's where I felt the story of the home should begin.

that comes into the home, the better. This home faces north, so I added windows on the south side to flood the living room with natural light. This house also presented an opportunity to utilize crossing light, which intersects with the main lighting from multiple angles and heights to create warmth and beautiful light and shadow throughout the day.

New construction allows you to start from scratch, but it can often feel soulless and predictable. It was important for me to think through the details of this home so I could ensure that the newness never felt cold. To add warmth and interest, I selected an aggregate concrete flooring with customized colored pebbles mixed in. After the concrete is poured, the top layer is ground down to expose the stones. The process adds amazing texture and character to the entire space. The browns and earth tones of the pebbles make what would otherwise be sterile, gray concrete warm and interesting.

The wood, concrete, rocks, and glass are all organic materials. They brought a warm yet timeless feel to this newly built home, reflecting what I think is a perfect mix of modern elements and timeless design.

A quick coat of black spray paint gave this thrift-store wire shelving unit new life and made it a perfect place to display a curated vignette of vintage radios.

Our riverside family retreat has clean lines and a modern feel that complements the natural surroundings. The wood, black metal, and oversize windows will feel stylish even as trends come and go.

The presence of so much natural light in this entryway allows for huge statement pieces, such as the aggregate concrete floors and floating staircase. The glass panels in the front door allow for even more light to enter. The wooden door, the wicker basket, and the rattan pendant help to soften this area and create a welcoming entrance.

OPPOSITE: This low-profile sectional offsets the bold, dark leather, which complements the room's metal accents (on the chairs, sliding doors, and fireplace ledge). The dramatic contrast between the two-story ceilings and the lower furniture keeps sight lines clear and balances the focus among all the room's features.

ABOVE: Making unique choices, like repurposing this metal container to pot a houseplant, can add extra interest in unexpected ways.

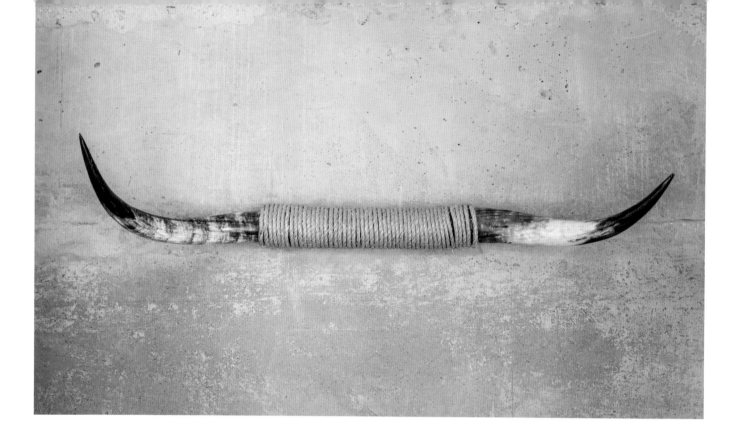

ABOVE: My mom bought this bull's horn for me for my fortieth birthday. I love how cool this piece looks on the concrete wall.

RIGHT: Bringing the outdoors in can add life to a space in simple ways. This tree stump acts as a side table in the upstairs living space.

OPPOSITE: These pendant lights originally hung in a nearby cathedral. We found them at a thrift store and then painted them black to contrast with the wood interior that shines through when they're illuminated.

A wood backsplash is an unconventional but impactful choice here. Wood is usually avoided near a stove top because heat and food ruin it, but with the correct finish, it can actually be durable and easy to maintain.

ABOVE: Bringing in wall art is a simple way to add personality to any space. In this dining room, I commissioned this custom painting with bright colors to break up the dark hues in the rest of the kitchen.

OPPOSITE: This giant ceramic pot has an ancient look, and the tall branches lead the eye upward. The visual diversity of color, texture, and height breaks up the monochrome counters and backsplash.

The custom design of the
floating concrete stairs,
while beautiful, presented
some logistical challenges,
including our having to add a
concrete wall for support. But
the end result, with a special
reading nook in the open
space under the stairs, was
worth the trouble.

The custom neon sign above the bed is on a dimmer, which makes it functional for a bedroom. I had it designed with a message that was meaningful to me, and I love that it adds a little bit of whimsy and personality to the room. I also think of neon as quintessential Americana.

OPPOSITE: This 1960s rocking chair, with its woven frame and leather cushions, brings a touch of sophistication and history to the main bedroom. The pair of nightstands were a thrift-store find. We sanded them down to reveal the original blond wood.

ABOVE: The custom vanities are made from white oak, which gives the bathroom a clean, modern look. The soapstone countertop is durable and adds a beautiful but simple contrast to the bathroom, which makes it feel warm in a way that a full stone vanity and countertop might not.

The focal point of my home office is the vintage shelving, which was found at a thrift store for $12.99. It became the perfect place to display personal collections.

Mid-Century **Modern**

I n 2006, my sister, Sarah, who was living in Southern California at the time, was considering moving back to Boise but wanted to find the right house, so she started searching online for new listings that were coming on the market. She spotted a mid-century modern house that appeared to have been untouched since 1963, when it was built. The architect who designed the home lived there. His purposeful design was apparent in every detail.

Sarah and her family fell in love with the potential and originality of this home and bought it. Soon after, I received a phone call asking if I would help remove the floor-to-ceiling brown bamboo wallpaper that had been hung across the entire house (I guess we can chalk that up to a "fun" family project). When the renovation started in earnest, the first goal was to figure out how to bring in light materials to contrast with the dark stone used throughout the house—on the floors, the walls,

and the exterior. Other priorities included modifying the kitchen, adding an en suite bathroom, and transforming the backyard into an extended living area. Most of the natural elements remained: the tongue-and-groove ceiling, the flagstone floor, and the fireplace, one of the most stunning I've ever seen. In the end, my sister and brother-in-law made the home comfortable and livable without compromising or erasing the original details.

Mid-century design prioritizes bringing natural elements from outside into the interior space, and that's exactly what the architect accomplished with this home.

An entryway is a great spot for introducing the feel that will be carried through the rest of the home. In this case, mixing multiple textural elements—such as the stone flooring, the wood credenza, the foraged greenery, the brass candlesticks, the ceramic lamp, and the vintage books—is a great way to accomplish that. With so many items in this space, the center art piece grounds the composition.

My favorite thing about mid-century modern style is not so much that it's retro but that it emphasizes indoor/outdoor living, clean lines, and warmth.

The home's entryway is an atrium featuring oversize plants, vaulted wooden ceilings, and floor-to-ceiling windows that bring abundant natural light to the space. Inside, as is also customary for mid-century homes, is a large open space meant for gathering. Oftentimes mid-century modern houses feature smaller bedrooms and larger living areas, which make the home more practical for entertaining and more conducive to family time.

Sometimes people feel that, when decorating a mid-century modern home, everything in it needs to be mid-century modern, too. I don't agree. It's important to have nods to the period, but it's just as important to allow your personal taste and preferences to come through. Never be afraid to mix different design styles.

In this home, I particularly love the low-profile sofas, which befit the era's style. They're new, making them feel modern at the same time and bringing balance to the architecture and furnishings.

If you try to use only furniture from the same era as the house, it can often feel dated. When purchasing core pieces, whether side chairs, sofas, rugs, or credenzas, make sure they work well together. Then layer in the smaller objects and accessories among the bigger pieces.

My favorite thing about mid-century modern style is not so much that it's retro but that it emphasizes indoor/outdoor living, clean lines, and warmth. Homes built in the late nineteenth century and in the earlier part of the twentieth century are often ornate and intricate; in the mid-twentieth century, design became more simplified and streamlined. It inspired the less-is-more ideal, and I've come to uphold that notion.

In this mid-century modern home, it was vital to find classic pieces, such as the chair, side table, and lamp—all from the 1950s—that matched the era of the house.

The warm tones of the natural stone and brick, along with the double-door entry, are quintessential mid-century modern design elements. There's no doubt about when this home was built.

ABOVE: While the custom detailed metalwork that separates the entryway from the great room isn't necessary, it is a beautiful way to begin to tell the story of this home's unique design.

OPPOSITE: The oversize double entry doors speak to the greatness of this mid-century modern home, despite its humble exterior. The detail in the woodwork creates a beautiful symmetry that makes a strong statement and adds to the natural curb appeal, or how the home looks from the street.

PREVIOUS: Low furniture paired with tall ceilings makes any space feel less fussy and more livable.

ABOVE: This open shelf exemplifies the practicality of 1950s design.

OPPOSITE: The white palette allows for the opportunity to mix in color through collections and heirlooms, which, in turn, bring personality to a room, as they do in this vignette.

Bringing outdoor foliage indoors gives vibrancy, color, and fragrance to your space, and it doesn't cost a thing. Look no further than your own backyard for the best details.

This stone wall is a classic example of how natural elements were worked into classic mid-century modern design. It has a major impact in the space and adds warmth and texture to the room.

ABOVE: This mid-century modern lamp pairs well with the brass and the vintage books and elevates the feel of the room. You can get creative with your bookends; for example, I'm using this candle as a bookend.

RIGHT: One way to incorporate bold color into your home is to install artwork. It adds life and personality, and you don't have to be committed to it forever.

One of the simplest ways to bring character into your space is to repurpose antique items, such as this beautiful blanket, which was handmade and used for generations in a small Indian village and now has pride of place framed above the console.

OPPOSITE: This small atrium brings the outdoors inside and is one of the best things to come out of mid-century modern design.

ABOVE: One of the main debates in this renovation—a common question in current design—was whether to paint the wood trim throughout the house. In this case, keeping the warm wood tones was the right choice, and it creates beautiful contrast within each area.

ABOVE: This is Oscar. Oscar loves the pool. Who doesn't?

OPPOSITE: A simple firepit and repurposed tree stumps were an inexpensive way to create a functional outdoor space and expand the living area.

Mountain **Modern**

Sometimes homes are renovated into something they were never intended to be, and that was the case with this mid-century house, originally built in 1963. It was updated and given a farmhouse/cabin feel in the early 2000s, which left it in a strange design limbo. The home featured five different kinds of wood and random Shaker touches everywhere. The house didn't quite know what it was, but it definitely had the potential to return to its former glory and to be modernized at the same time.

Thankfully, the original 1960s stone fireplace, a quintessential mid-century feature, was untouched in the farmhouse remodel. This fireplace, situated in the center of the home, had the ability to be a show-stopping focal point.

Mid-century architecture was designed to allow for flow and natural light, but the first thing I noticed in this home was that the spaces *didn't* flow: the kitchen was closed off from the dining room, the dining room was closed off from the living room, and the living room was closed off from the entrance. There wasn't even enough space for a proper table in the kitchen.

My job as a designer is ultimately to serve the clients, so even though I immediately wanted to open everything up, the first thing I had to do was ask *What does the family need?* What did we need to do to make the house workable for them? How could we achieve that with design and flow? In this case, completely changing the entire layout was the only feasible way to accomplish those goals.

In this classic modern mountain home, the fireplace became the cornerstone of the design and remodel. The beauty of the detailed craftsmanship in the stonework makes the fireplace especially striking.

By thinking outside the box and making some key design changes, this once awkward house was transformed from a disjointed space that was ill-suited to spending time together into an open, spacious, beautiful mid-century mountain home.

Typically, removing a bedroom wouldn't be considered in a remodel plan, but the bedroom on the main floor was the cause of the house's constricted flow. We decided to demolish the room from floor to ceiling and turn the space into the home's first real dining room. That one decision completely changed the living dynamic for this growing family.

Opening up this space provided new design opportunities, and one of our favorite choices was to install a concrete feature wall. A feature wall is an achievable DIY project in which one wall in a space is given a different surface treatment to make it stand out. In other homes I've used wallpaper, wood accents, patterns, or even bold paint colors. In this home, we added a skim coat of concrete, which brought in texture and a natural feel while simultaneously modernizing the mid-century design. For cohesiveness, I installed concrete pendant lights above the island and a concrete sink in the powder bath. Coordinating design elements in different spaces is a simple way to tie the overall design together.

One of the focus items of this project was to improve the curb appeal. The exterior paint was outdated, and the landscape was overgrown in some areas and dead in others. Because the home was surrounded by nature and evergreens, I suggested going with a bold black exterior to make an impactful statement and provide a stark contrast to the naturally wooded area. The wooden front door softens the entrance; I love adding wooden front doors, because they create a welcoming feel.

By thinking outside the box and making some key design changes, this once awkward house was transformed from a disjointed space that was ill-suited to spending time together into an open, spacious, beautiful mid-century mountain home.

Even though there's a lot of wood here, it doesn't feel too cabin-y because the clean lines and horizontal beams bring a modern symmetry to the space.

Before its renovation, this home was worn and outdated. The fresh black paint revitalized it.

When choosing interior pieces for your house, it's important to think not only about function and comfort but also about color scheme and how new pieces will connect with materials that are already in the home. Here, the sofa and rug particularly complement the muted surrounding tones.

A simple way to add life and color to an otherwise monochromatic area is to incorporate houseplants. Snake plants, like the one shown here, are among the easiest plants to keep alive. They're also relatively inexpensive.

Styling a space comes down to your unique point of view and what inspires you. I've learned that incorporating distinctive and personal items is what ultimately makes your house a home.

ABOVE: Adding a skim coat of concrete on the entire interior wall added texture, color, and depth in an uncommon and inexpensive way.

OPPOSITE: The space you see here was originally three separate rooms: one for living, one for dining, and one for cooking. By removing the walls and adding a structural beam spanning the living room, this area morphed into a complete open concept.

White, wood tones, and black is a classic combination. It's also the perfect canvas for mixing and matching your personal style in any season of life. In this case, a colorful woven rug brings personality and soul to the kitchen.

OPPOSITE: Stacked tile, a pattern in which each tile is set directly above the one below it, is common in mid-century design. Don't let open shelving in a kitchen limit you to kitchen items.

ABOVE: You can never go wrong with a night in, entertaining friends. Whether fun cocktails or cups of hot cocoa are on the menu, cheers! The blue-based lamp, blue inlaid tray, fresh nuts and flowers, and cocktail-hour glassware create the vibe for a perfect evening.

Natural light and open spaces exude all things mid-century, and adding an oversize island is a modern touch that works with the original design.

Symmetry is pleasing to the eye. This modern double vanity is a perfect example of symmetrical design done well.

OPPOSITE: After a long day, there are few things that bring more joy than a hot bath. A soaking tub doesn't have to be the traditional white. Look into other color options to incorporate into your space, like this tub with a black exterior.

ABOVE: These original 1950s floating side tables fit seamlessly into the minimalist design of this primary bedroom, while also adding texture and contrast to the space.

The painted window trim unifies the room, connecting it to the bold feature wall. The black also stands out against the classic white walls in a cost-effective yet refined way.

PART II

Natural
&
ORGANIC

love natural and organic elements like stone, millwork, weaving, clay, ceramic, or brick because they're at once timeless and warm. They also have character. Even with something as simple as stone, you'll see unique details, intricacies, and imperfections. Natural materials, I think, bring to us the serenity of the natural world. Using those materials indoors actually connects us to the outside.

Timber and Love's Boise headquarters are located just a few feet from the Ridge to Rivers greenbelt and the Boise River. The rustle of leaves on the trees, the water rippling over the rocks, and the changing colors of the seasons inspire me. Being able to bring even a small portion of that authenticity into work spaces or living spaces provides the balance and unfussiness of nature.

As we explore these next three houses, my goal is for you to be inspired to explore the possibilities of bringing what you love about the outdoors into your home. Natural and organic elements can be foundational to your design and help foster a connection to the surrounding beauty wherever you live.

The Firehouse

This unique 1911 property, situated in the historic North End of Boise, was the third firehouse built in the city. The first floor housed a barn for horse-drawn fire engines, and the upstairs contained the living quarters for the firefighters on shift and included bedrooms and a kitchen. When the bell sounded to signal an emergency, the firefighters could quickly access the wagons by using the fire pole that connected the upstairs to the downstairs. The horses were trained to hook themselves into the wagon when they heard the alarm. The station was in service for about forty years, but it fell into disrepair in the 1950s when the city built a new station. In 2017, the city of Boise decided to sell this historic firehouse at auction, knowing that renovating it and bringing it up to code would be a massive undertaking. As a kid, I walked past this building every day, and when I heard it was for sale, I knew I wanted to restore it. I was thrilled to find we'd put in the winning bid.

To restore the property with historical integrity, I referenced pictures from the early 1900s. The Shaker shingles, the stucco exterior, and the barn doors were all original to the firehouse. Inside, there were oversize custom-built doors that had been covered in Sheetrock, and throughout the wood was caked in layers of paint that had accumulated over the years. After weeks of stripping and sanding, the doors were restored to their original glory, and the property started to come back to life.

Below the drop ceiling in the area that was once the barn, we found original lath and plaster. It was perfectly imperfect: discolored and raw. I left it exposed to highlight the warmth and history of the texture. But keeping the lath and plaster meant we couldn't cut into

Restoring original details, such as these historic barn doors, is a wonderful way to stay true to the heritage of a project while bringing natural, organic elements back to life in a beautiful, noticeable way.

To restore the property with historical integrity, I referenced pictures from the early 1900s. The Shaker shingles, the stucco exterior, and the barn doors were all original to the firehouse. Inside . . . the wood was caked in layers of paint that had accumulated over the years. After weeks of stripping and sanding, the doors were restored to their original glory, and the property started to come back to life.

it to hide wiring or piping behind it, so I decided to expose the copper metal piping throughout the building.

I loved the firehouse's original fireplace, which felt like it had been there for hundreds of years. It didn't have a hearth, however, so I sourced flagstone— a timeless material—to radiate heat back into the room and to match the era of the original building. The fire pole had been removed, but we purchased a new one, made of brass, and aged it with salt and vinegar to give it an appropriate patina. By using flagstone and a natural element like brass, we were able to create an organic feel in the space.

Downstairs, I sourced the green enamel pendant lights from thrift stores and vintage boutiques. One even turned up in an old barn. There are fourteen lights on the ground floor, and each one is slightly different. Designers can sometimes fixate on making things perfect, but allowing imperfections creates beauty, too.

Upstairs, we started from scratch. Again, I wanted to design something timeless but also true to the building's previous story—and because the space would

become a short-term rental property, I needed it to feel elevated, too. We added an upstairs fireplace, built to be consistent with the one downstairs, and installed a brand-new kitchen with a moveable island. I found an old metal worktable, removed the original top, and replaced it with a custom Copper Dune Leather Granite in a honed finish, which immediately tied together the copper finishes throughout the building. We put the table on casters so we could move it around depending on what was happening in the kitchen and how many people were there. With each day of the renovation, and the introduction of each new element—or the exaltation of what had been there before—the soul came back into this restored and repurposed firehouse. I love the way you can feel the history of the firehouse, and yet also see that it has a dual function.

Unique lighting adds character and personality to any room. Here I worked with my son Elias, who had an idea for a light fixture. It came to life as an oversize copper geometric pendant hung over this reclaimed farm table.

The vintage metal wood-burning fireplace set on natural stone is the focal point of the living room. The furniture, with its organic tones and worn accent pieces, creates a lived-in atmosphere that makes a beautifully designed space still feel accessible.

OPPOSITE: Choosing vintage furniture, rather than purchasing new pieces, adds character without sacrificing functionality. The rattan back of these dining chairs provides visual interest while contributing to the natural design style.

ABOVE: Although this stove isn't original to the firehouse, the natural patina and organic elements make it feel like it's been there since the early 1900s.

A hallmark of good design is the ability to relate different pieces without finding perfect matches. While this open floor plan is filled with a variety of beautiful furniture and accents, they are carefully placed to work together to make the space interesting but not overwhelming.

When creating different living spaces in the same home, it's important to include similar elements so that the space feels cohesive. Here, an additional vintage fireplace surrounded with stone, along with wood tones and natural details carried in from the bigger living room, makes this space feel like part of the overall design while allowing it to maintain its identity as a space of its own.

ABOVE: Choosing pieces that speak to you, much like this worn flag, can tell both your story and the story of the home, and it always makes the environment uniquely yours.

OPPOSITE: Including details, like this vintage popcorn popper, is a fun way to add life to any space, proving that even upscale design doesn't have to take itself too seriously.

TOP LEFT: Searching thrift stores for a variety of books with beautiful covers is not only a fun weekend activity but also a great way to curate decor that's both interesting and conversational.

TOP RIGHT: Introducing a lighter wood tone on this functional entryway bench fills a practical need in a way that feels special.

RIGHT: I was so excited when I was able to purchase this firehouse because I knew I could carry on a part of our family's story. Here's a picture of my grandpa, Hank Sabatasso, serving in the Los Angeles Fire Department.

A natural and organic design style always includes furniture pieces that ground the space. The organic feel of this antique wood dresser provides a perfect spot to hang this bold tapestry and group thrift store finds.

Textiles are an important part of design, and your choices can completely change the feel of a room. In this bedroom, the clean cotton bedding and white shades, which filter the light but don't block it, work together to highlight the amazing natural light in the space.

OPPOSITE: Providing strong contrast through textures and colors allows your space to simultaneously feel bold and elevated.

ABOVE: We chose not to reglaze the bathtub's exterior finish in order to display the natural patina that accumulated throughout the course of its life. The tub is a reminder of the blending of old and new in the home.

This is a small but functional kitchen. The island sits on casters so it can be moved around to accommodate the groups of people who inevitably hang out there, and the fridge is set into the wall, helping to maximize the small space.

Vintage light fixtures can add interest and soul to any space. This classic art deco schoolhouse light brought the perfect warmth and character to the kitchen.

ABOVE: Mixing new and old is a great technique for making a space feel lived-in. Here, the clean, white tile and copper-infused countertops contrast with the vintage lamp and the photos providing a link to this property's history.

LEFT: Even everyday items can become special when displayed intentionally. The patina on these copper pots provides a natural contrast with the simple white subway tile.

La Casetta

n Italian, *la Casetta* means "the Cottage." My sister Katie and her husband, Doug, purchased this 1980s kit home with the intention of turning it into a short-term rental. Katie's original vision for the house was to give it a simple, laid-back European feel. The home came alive in the details. They were sourced and curated with the intention of creating a welcoming, but still functional, home.

After World War II, kit homes were abundant. They were prefabricated, and could be erected quickly and easily. They were created en masse, so the floor plans and features were standardized and simplified. As a result, Katie's house didn't have innate character or charm, with the exception of some of the built-in kitchen cabinets. So, we brought in some carefully chosen pieces, such as the vintage chesterfield sofa and the tree stump extracted from the backyard and repurposed as the base of a coffee table, to give the home its identity and quiet sophistication.

In the bathroom, we removed the laminate flooring and replaced it with thin brick, which is reminiscent of a European cobblestone path—the sort of thing you'd find in a dreamy Italian village. We whitewashed the brick to create a neutral tone and arranged it in a chevron pattern to add panache and identity to the space.

Overall, the colors and tones throughout are muted

Mixing unique materials and textures adds intrigue to any room. Here, the worn leather mixes with the marble and the handwoven pillow to bring depth to the room.

Overall, the colors and tones throughout are muted and neutral. That doesn't mean the home can't be colorful—the vibrancy comes from the details. Pairing bright colors with more neutral ones creates a peaceful presence.

and neutral. That doesn't mean the home can't be colorful—the vibrancy comes from the details. Pairing bright colors with more neutral ones creates a peaceful presence. For example, the living room area rug has a red and green pattern and is enhanced by the red pillows and books, but the room is balanced by the cream blanket, the brown leather couches, and the wooden furniture. The textures create intrigue in the space and attract attention to the colors. Meanwhile, the woven jute in the ottoman, the braided fabric in the blanket, and the natural bark on the coffee table add soul to the room and contribute to the curated and thoughtful design.

Nearly every light fixture and accessory came from a secondhand store or a flea market. Their scuffs and patina give the space the lived-in feel of a cottage. Mixing and matching elements, such as the vintage light set on a metal bucket instead of a traditional nightstand and the stone horse with a vintage rug thrown over it like a saddle blanket, made the home feel quaint, which was exactly what Katie wanted for it.

Lighting choices can change an entire room. Choosing an unconventional lamp for this bright, cheery bedroom gives it a more lived-in, soulful feel.

With a space that has this much natural light, it's important to make smart choices with window coverings. Choosing drapes in an organic, light-colored fabric will allow the natural light to come into the room while still creating some privacy. Decorating this room with different sofas tied together the carefully chosen accessories.

TOP LEFT: The front door of a home can foreshadow what's inside.

TOP RIGHT: Greenery is key to natural design. Although the task can be daunting, choosing plants that work in your climate and your particular room is an important part of curating the space.

RIGHT: No detail is too small in design. Intentional styling allows you to introduce textural intrigue and vibrancy through found objects. Here, these books provide soul and color.

OPPOSITE: When furnishing your space, there's always room for personal preference. Although this buffet was originally meant to serve in a dining area, placing it in the living space is a smart way to include a statement piece with a warm, natural finish, and to provide extra storage.

This cottage has quaint details that you don't often see in new construction, such as this niche in the kitchen. It makes for practical storage, as well as a place to display vintage books and an unexpected houseplant.

ABOVE: Accessories add character to any space. Finding functional pieces is a bonus. Here, the worn cutting board, a relatively small thing, really exudes a natural and organic feel.

LEFT: Fresh flowers are an easy way to bring understated beauty to any space. In this case, three simple, whimsical arrangements make this corner of the kitchen feel extra special.

OPPOSITE: The clean lines of the white cabinets and countertops, contrasted with the natural wood floors and this vintage step stool, work together perfectly in this quaint kitchen.

ABOVE & RIGHT: Ordinary, practical items can live out in the open on your countertop. Everyday living means that not everything has to be put away.

ABOVE: Bringing in items with different colors and finishes transforms a blank slate into a charming space.

OPPOSITE: While most of this kitchen is simple and white, it was important to add something a little different, which we did with this natural-finish shelf, a perfect place to store everyday items.

In this bedroom, the simple tapestry and the solid white drapes create a light and airy feel. The wall-mounted sconces create space on the bedside tables for these lovely fresh flowers.

ABOVE: This unique cast-iron horse bench is an unexpected item that adds an established, European sensibility to the room.

OPPOSITE: Originally part of a dining set, this chair was passed down through several generations. The table and other chairs no longer worked for the family, but they wanted to keep the memory of the family dining table, so this chair was repurposed as a bedroom side chair.

OPPOSITE: A fun way to add personality to an otherwise simple bathroom is by combining multiple textural objects within the same tonality. This space is styled with a vintage woven basket, a clay vase, and a stone jewelry box, whose warm, neutral tones pair well together.

ABOVE: Utilizing brick, rather than traditional tile, for the bathroom floor is an unusual choice, but it gives the room a charming and organic feel, reminiscent of European styling.

The Eclectic Home

Someone with *eclectic taste* has a variety of stylistic interests and uses them in an original or eccentric way. My wife and I purchased this 1930s house with original classic architecture and some unique details and transformed it into the most eclectic home I've ever designed. I wanted it to feel lived-in without feeling old, comfortable yet quirky. We brought in collections we'd curated over time and as we traveled to different continents.

When beginning a project, it's good practice to create a blank canvas where your ideas can come to life. Painting all of the walls a lighter color establishes consistency and a canvas for all that's to come. I prefer to use warm whites on the walls, and that's exactly what I did in this home. The walls had a thick lath texture that I actually decided to keep because it added warmth. I mixed it with the new white paint to achieve the fresh, clean look I was aiming for.

We swapped the old carpet for a classic pinewood floor. Pine is a soft wood with a rustic warmth that elevates a space without making it feel overly sophisticated. Its natural feel is welcoming. Here, that feeling is enhanced by the beautiful brick fireplace. The cost-effective option of central heating made fireplaces less necessary in American homes built after the 1950s,

Styling this home with vintage furnishings and classic finds brings a lot of soul and interest to an otherwise simplistic starter home.

I appreciate and understand a variety of styles, and prefer not to design in one singular way. That allows for personality, rather than a cookie-cutter look.

when central electric heating became more common, but the warmth fireplaces provide, both physically and emotionally, has helped them remain a popular element in American home design. The image of a family gathering around a fireplace or cozying up near the fire with some good books evokes classic Americana nostalgia.

I appreciate and understand a variety of styles, and prefer not to design in one singular way. That allows for personality, rather than a cookie-cutter look. For this home in particular I gathered some of my favorite objects and furnishings, like vintage license plates, repurposed mid-century chairs, and an antique banquette that I had been holding on to for years. I used old potato sacks, whose burlap anchors the space while still allowing in light, for the window coverings. Together, these items now coexist and give this home its unique and eclectic identity. Mixing and matching is truly an art form, and there's no right or wrong way to do it.

The eclectic design of this room is all about practical living. If you don't have room for a bookcase, don't be afraid to stack!

I found two accent chairs from a thrift store for this living room. The fabric was originally pink linen, but I had them reupholstered in buffalo plaid, a classic American pattern and a staple of fashion and interior design.

OPPOSITE: In this corner, the natural wood of the tabletop and the vintage light and clock pair perfectly with the weathered, industrial look of these antique license plates, which add a local flair.

ABOVE: Placing a thermos on a mantel might seem out of place; however, when creatively arranged, it becomes a unique bookend. Using items differently than their intended use is one of my favorite ways to make a room feel unique and interesting.

In the main living space, the warm wood framing and the leather sofa bring out the tones of the other details, such as the chest next to the entrance and the black fabric of the tapestry seen through the doorway. The tall cactus calls attention to the coved ceilings. Overall, the room comes together through the various masculine touches.

ABOVE: Pairing organic textiles and natural details can create interest in an understated way. The bold colors in this tapestry contrasts heavily with the neutral backdrop, drawing your eye.

OPPOSITE: Choosing plants with interesting textures, like this cactus, can add life and color to a room and, with varied textures, makes the design feel unique.

This space is another example of how you can style a room in a way that creates a particular feeling upon entering. The different grains and tones of wood, textiles, and casually arranged books and knickknacks give this space its eclectic yet comfortable feel.

The King Edward cigar boxes add a nostalgic feel to the vignette of this arched niche. The antique candlestick sconces on either side frame the display and add to the warmth and appeal of the composition.

Kitchens don't have to be shiny and new to be beautiful. In this space, the original layout works within the overall design of the home, and is referenced in the arch detail over the window. Sticking with a neutral color palette throughout keeps the kitchen simple yet practical.

OPPOSITE: You don't have to throw away that old stove! I've heard it said that everything comes back around. A little vintage charm can go a long way.

ABOVE: In a kitchen with limited countertop space, clever shelving can be a lifesaver. It can also add charm, like providing a place for these red-handled scissors and this natural-bristle brush.

ABOVE: One of the joys of curating is the opportunity to use unexpected statement pieces, like this lion statuette that brings a strong presence to the room.

OPPOSITE: These vintage theater seats are unconventional but very practical, as they add extra seating to the room.

OPPOSITE: Working with a smaller space doesn't always mean you have to design in a minimal way. In this bathroom, I leaned into the tight area with a gallery wall abundant with old paintings.

ABOVE: When designing in a bedroom that isn't spacious, it's especially important to maximize the light. One option is to choose a strong, statement headboard that doesn't block the light.

PART III

Classic
&
COZY

hen I envision a place that's classic and cozy, I see something that feels timeless, beautiful, and right-for-the-moment all at once. Trends come and go and styles change, but a timeless place always feels right.

One of the things that classic design and cozy elements can often bring is a sense of warmth and security, which isn't always found only in a cozy blanket. After my wife and I had our first two kids, we knew we wanted to adopt children, and one of the first things we thought about was making sure that they would feel comfortable in our home. The children, having lived their lives in orphanages until then, were coming from places that weren't secure, and we wanted to ensure that they felt both emotionally stable and physically comfortable, and that they had a safe place to grow. It's amazing to me that design can play such a big role in that.

Cozy can be found in tones, textures, furnishings, and architectural elements. The difference between a warm fabric and a stiff, cold leather sofa can affect the environment you're trying to create. Setting the mood through lighting, warm wall tones, or natural elements like wood makes a place feel cozy. So does a fireplace, of course.

We live in a society where something is always trending, and we can easily get pulled into design styles that come and go quickly. A classic design, however, stands the test of time. Craftsman and cottage-style homes are typical examples of classic designs: they use natural materials, simple patterns, and timeless finishes.

Classic **Craftsman**

My kids have always loved visiting their grandma's house, so this house, to us, is a place of warmth, comfort, and memories. There are always cookies baking when we arrive, and nothing beats spending time in the kitchen together. We also spend a lot of time sitting around the living room fireplace. It's constructed of the same sandstone as the house's exterior and is the focal point of the space.

The kitchen has beautiful light wood butcher-block countertops and vintage appliances that make it a special space of its own. The craftsman style is evident throughout, with the pronounced case molding and the wood-paned windows, but the first thing that attracts me to the home is the welcoming front door. The wood contrasts with the bright white trim, and the window boxes full of red geraniums stand out against the warm, blue exterior of the house. The sandstone block that frames the exterior was quarried over a hundred years ago from the hills of Table Rock, a nearby Boise landmark, and are prevalent in homes in the North End neighborhood, as well as the Idaho Capitol building.

In a classic style, simple details make a strong impact, like this beautiful bouquet.

For as long as I can remember, my mom has always had fresh flowers in her home, and now it's something my wife and I do in our house as well. It adds life to our home that can't be created by material objects.

The pronounced entry and the cute front porch are, to me, quintessential Americana. They suggest a community, a neighborhood where people gather.

One of the things I appreciate about this classic home are the old fir wood floors. They have history, and through the years I've seen these floors come back to life many times after showing signs of wear and tear. Fir is a soft wood, but it has character, and, like all wood floors, it can be refinished repeatedly. One story is left behind, and a new one starts with the fresh refinish. It's symbolic of the seasons of life that we all experience.

This traditional craftsman home is the perfect setting for timeless and established pieces. Finding unique antique furniture, like dressers, side chairs, and coffee tables, and incorporating it into your design helps make a home feel at once classic and cozy. Quality furnishings last and elevate the space. And a chair with a modern silhouette, for example, paired with an antique coffee table helps balance the two styles.

For as long as I can remember, my mom has always had fresh flowers in her home, and now it's something my wife and I do in our house as well. It adds life to our home that can't be created by material objects.

The rich cream walls reflect the natural light that pours in, adding to the warm feel of the room.

The details in this craftsman home amplify its classic feel. From the rich blue exterior with its white trim and geranium-filled window boxes to the classic stone details and thoughtful landscaping, this home is rich with curb appeal.

ABOVE: The fireplace is the heart of this home. With its natural, locally sourced stone and vintage insert, it makes a statement even with minimal decor around it.

OPPOSITE: Furniture with natural, warm wood tones and classic lines makes a home feel intentionally traditional.

What I love most about this room is the light coming from different directions and the way it hits the furniture; light creates beauty.

Large dining tables can, surprisingly, work well in a small space like this one. Here, the windows allow light to stream through and make the room feel open rather than crowded.

Wall art doesn't always have to be framed and arranged for a formal feel. Finding themes that speak to you and curating a collection, such as this arrangement of floral prints, is a wonderful way to add a casual but beautiful focal point to the room.

ABOVE: An overstated floral arrangement placed on a classic furniture piece is a simple way to elevate the feel of a design, while leaving room for seasonal changes.

LEFT: Layering found objects creates special vignettes and points of interest in a space. Staggering objects behind one another and using a variety of heights can add depth to small spaces.

ABOVE: The antique leaded glass brings personality to the kitchen. Antiques can go in any room.

OPPOSITE: This charming vintage desk and chair provide a spot for displaying found objects while also creating a useful space.

OPPOSITE: This original clawfoot tub and the penny hex tile complement the classic white subway tile in this bathroom, while the colorful print of the shower curtain adds elegance and warmth.

ABOVE: The primary bedroom showcases a vintage metal headboard paired with textured linens, alongside a warm wood night table with classic lines. Finished off with a floral arrangement to continue the floral theme of the home, this space is inviting and relaxing while also being fresh and beautiful.

Cozy Cottage

We had the privilege of working with a young couple, the Sundells, on our HGTV show *Outgrown*. Their 1935 cottage had been in the family for years, but as their family grew, the house they loved wasn't practical anymore, yet it was so full of history and memories that they couldn't bear to leave. The focus of this project was to make the small house workable for a family of four and create a space the kids could grow into, all while maintaining the history of this cottage they had grown to love.

The original entrance to the home led right into a set of stairs. The fireplace was smack in the middle of the house, which made creating flow challenging. It was original to the home and had character, so we didn't want to move or obscure it; the flow needed to revolve around this classic feature. Not surprisingly, the layout was compartmentalized. The kitchen, living area, and bedroom were all located on the first floor in three small, separate areas. There was no dining room, and the kitchen had very little counter space.

Adding square footage was the only solution to keep this cottage in the family and make it functional for

Fireplaces are a staple of classic and cozy design. The brick detail and wooden mantel, along with neutral-colored accents in various organic materials, draw your focus from any spot in the room.

Adding square footage was the only solution to keep this cottage in the family and make it functional for their future. So, we did something a little radical: The primary bedroom, which was located on the first floor adjacent to the living room, became a new dining area.

their future. So, we did something a little radical: The primary bedroom, which was located on the first floor adjacent to the living room, became a new dining area. That improved the flow on the first floor.

But, of course, we couldn't just dispense with the bedroom. So, to replace it, we added an addition onto the side of the home that included a new bedroom, a full bath, and a walk-in closet. We wanted the addition to feel like it fit with the original part of the house, so we added vaulted ceilings and wooden beams, which also made the room feel larger and added warmth. An indented arch within the bedroom wall created a built-in headboard feature and carried the arch motif throughout the home.

We relocated the entrance, added a new mudroom and dining room, built a breakfast bar, and created space for yet another bedroom. The house ultimately felt more expansive and open—and it was!

Seeing the kids running through the house with plenty of space to play and knowing the parents now had the foundation of a functional home was the best reward of all.

Mixing textures and finishes in a room works well in the classic and cozy style. In this dining space, I added a curated gallery wall to highlight the client's personality and story.

The sofa's warm leather, the cowhide rug, the mantel, and the unusual hood with its wooden vent make the space cozy, and the elements flow from area to area, bringing the place together and making it feel cohesive and not siloed.

OPPOSITE: The arches on the hutch echo the arches throughout the home. Once used to display fine china, this piece is now a spot to display books and collected items.

ABOVE: This adorable wooden writing desk fits perfectly in a small space that otherwise wouldn't have been used for anything, and provides a home for the record player and a vintage book collection.

This kitchen is at once sophisticated and homey. The Shaker cabinets in crisp white are set off by the black subway tile and the naturally marbled black-and-white stone countertops. The colors and tones are classic and provide a base for bringing in the personal items that make the space your own.

ABOVE: Flea markets and thrift stores are great places to pick up gems like this antique kitchen scale. The bright sheen adds contrast to this otherwise dark corner of the kitchen.

LEFT: When shopping for antique books in thrift stores, search for books with similar color schemes but varying widths to create coordinated visual interest.

OPPOSITE: Using the same colors and materials in various spaces throughout a home makes it feel cohesive without duplicating design. This drop zone is a great example of how form and function work well together.

Although this bathroom is new, the classic details—such as the natural wood built-in storage cabinet and vanity, along with the white subway tile—create a relaxing space with clean lines and warm tones. The graphic detail in the flooring adds visual interest without overwhelming the space.

OPPOSITE: A cozy feel can be achieved in many different ways. Bringing in simple details, for example, can subtly enhance the feel of a room. Here, this healthy houseplant and these soft, flowy drapes pair with different textiles on the bed to make the room feel welcoming and cozy without adding too many items.

ABOVE: Highlighting architectural features with simple accessories will elevate a space in a classic way. These light and airy plants draw the eye to the arched detail above the bed in the new primary bedroom.

Crisp white linens and a chunky knit blanket continue the simple styling in this bright and cozy primary bedroom. Matching bedside tables with marble tops provide a canvas for displaying photographs and special details, finishing the design of this gorgeous space.

The bold wallpaper in this bathroom shows how to work graphic details that reflect personal style into the overall feel of a home. The arched vanity mirror and brass vase with fresh-cut flowers make this unique bathroom a showpiece.

Timeless Estate

This Spanish-inspired home is perfectly situated on multiple acres with the roaring Boise River just steps away. The land is surrounded by hundred-year-old trees, winding walking paths, and lush landscaping.

I've built new homes and remodeled others, but when this project came to me, I hadn't done many restorations. I was excited for the challenge of bringing the house back to life while preserving all the details, from the ninety-year-old kitchen tile to the original plaster on the walls. At the same time, we had to add modern amenities that would allow this home to function in the years to come.

In working on this restoration, one of the unique things we found was that this home had originally been heated by a geothermal radiant system, but at some point it was updated with a new forced-air heating unit for more efficiency. I thought the original radiators added a unique character, and since they were no longer being used to heat the home, we repurposed them into benches.

This house is all about hospitality and making the people in it feel welcome. It has four separate entrances: two leading into the dining room and two into the living room. All the entrances are connected by the front exterior courtyard. Clearly there were a lot of gatherings and events here. Two of these entrance doors open into the awe-inspiring living room, the true heart of the home. The large arched window stretches from one side of the room to the other, defining the room and allowing for abundant natural light. The soft curves of the arches invite you into the space and make the room feel intimate and cozy, while the coved ceilings, paired

This house is home to many dramatic details, such as the dark wood trim, original to the home, that provides a beautiful frame for the doorway into the bright, open kitchen.

A century old, the chandelier desperately needed some attention. So, my kids and I took a day to do just that. We removed every crystal and then cleaned and polished each and every one, restoring them to their original beauty.

with the gorgeous art deco glass sconces throughout the home, provide elegance and sophistication.

One of the characteristics of this home that we knew needed to be restored but also had to remain true to its original form was the array of wooden details, including the hardwood floors and the wood trim throughout. My goal was to bring these details back to the original richness and color that I can only imagine they had when they were first installed in the 1930s. The beauty of hardwood floors is they can often be brought back to life. To accomplish that, all the wood surfaces were meticulously sanded down and re-stained to bring back the original dark, classic finish that's typical of this era. One of the things I love about good design is that, instead of having to redo everything, oftentimes things can be brought back to life with nothing more than a fresh refinish.

One of the other features that really stood out to me was the beautiful chandelier in the dining room. A century old, it desperately needed some attention. So, my kids and I took a day to do just that. We removed every crystal and

then cleaned and polished each and every one, restoring them to their original beauty. Being a part of small restorations like this one can be a rewarding experience.

I would be remiss if I didn't talk about the charming kitchen. The penny hex tile that was laid nearly a century ago still looked as good as ever. And the original nook with the built-in benches and coved ceiling gave it a cozy charm that would be hard to replicate. The original features are a testament to the intricate design and attention to detail that went into making this house a home, and are integral pieces of this home's story and history. What's so amazing about classic design is the fact that nearly one hundred years later, this home still had so many beautiful and awe-inspiring features that we kept. It proves that classic design will always be timeless. Sometimes all it needs is a little bit of love to keep it enjoyable for generations to come.

In keeping with the art deco style, the metallic wallpaper in the dining room highlights this unique vintage chandelier. Its elegant and timeless design exemplifies the era of the 1930s.

The exterior of this Spanish-style home begins to tell its story. The tile roof and stucco exterior, along with the gas lanterns and wood-trimmed glass doors, are surrounded by lush landscaping and hint at the timelessness of this beautiful estate.

The abundant light in this room makes it possible to bring in dark tones without making the space feel small. Original wrought-iron drapery hardware and dark green drapes frame the wood windows.

ABOVE: This found vintage record player fits perfectly in this 1930s home.

OPPOSITE: A wooden plank atop the radiator creates additional seating, making the radiator not only even more functional but also stylish.

THE GREAT WEST

This original window is the focal point of the beautiful living area and offers picturesque views all year-round. The wood accents and arches throughout are warm and inviting.

Coming across an architectural detail that makes a statement is special. In this case, the original design of this massive window is so impactful that leaving the styling to a minimum gives it the attention it deserves.

OPPOSITE: This kitchen contains many nooks and niches that became special design moments. A collection of vintage mugs highlights this small alcove with color and texture.

ABOVE: I found this antique stove in perfect condition and knew it would work well in the bright white kitchen.

I showcased this unique penny tile by keeping the rest of the kitchen surfaces white; attention is immediately drawn to the spectacular original flooring in this space.

OPPOSITE: There's nothing quite as quaint as a built-in breakfast nook. With its vintage church pews and copper pendant light, this is where I would drink my coffee every morning.

ABOVE: With the beautiful natural light and the open window bringing in a fresh breeze, doing the dishes here isn't such a chore.

Keeping original hardware and unique design elements maintains the timeless details of the home. These touches can elevate your design and add soul in a way that isn't possible with new pieces.

Incorporating
vintage pieces into
an everyday-use
kitchen enlivens the
experience of the
space.

When renovating bathrooms, it's possible to modernize finishes in keeping with the home's original aesthetic. In this case, subway tile and the marble-top vanity stay true to the home's classic style.

Afterword

I want to thank you for taking this journey with me through these beautiful homes that, in some shape or form, represent classic Americana Soul. To me, what's so amazing about us as individuals is that we're all so unique. We all come from different places, with individual stories to tell, and our homes should reflect who we are as people—our own heritage, our own stories.

I love that a home can tell those stories. It can speak to what's important to you, what you love about life, and how you want to make other people feel in your home. Whether it's the pieces of furniture you choose, the artwork you hang, or the music you play in the background, you can create spaces where people feel welcome. A home, regardless of size or style, is a place of connection and love, a place where everyone who enters can have a voice. I believe everyone deserves to be heard, and everyone deserves to be loved.

I hope this book has inspired you in some way to be the best version of yourself and to open your arms, your homes, and your lives to love in a deeper, more intimate way. Thank you for letting me share my journey with you. It means so much to me to know that design can impact lives and intention can transform spaces and create places where memories, bonds, and connection can be built. That's the power of home. That's what I love about this work.

Nothing says home like a wood-burning fireplace. An environment where everybody feels comfortable and relaxed is ultimately where we all want to be.

Acknowledgments

I'm so thankful to everyone who gave their time, energy, and support to making this book a reality: Doris Cooper, Matthew Ryan, Frances Yackel, Molly Pieper, and Nick Teodoro and the team at Simon Element, thank you for believing in me and allowing me to share my story and work.

Brian Samuels and team, you are one of a kind! I appreciate your looking out for me and helping me accomplish my vision and goals.

To the team at Discovery and HGTV—Loren Ruch, Jane Latman, and Maggie Zeltner—thank you for believing in me and giving our family and business an incredible platform to share our story and work. I'm forever grateful.

Clint Robertson, thank you for being a friend who will always drop whatever you have going on to give a helping hand. I'm thankful for your friendship.

To the amazing team at Timber and Love, thank you for always being ready for an adventure and for supporting me every step of the way! Theresa T., thanks for helping me style and stage my way through these beautiful homes.

Danica Cusack, my photographer who captures design so well, and our amazing vendors like Anna Augusto and Paige Johnson, thank you for always being incredible partners and teammates.

Thank you to all the wonderful families and individuals who loaned your beautiful houses to us for this book. I am forever grateful to have worked on your homes and to have had the opportunity to create one-of-a-kind finished spaces.

To my loving family, thank you for supporting me every step of the way. To my mom, dad, sisters and brother, thank you for always being there to help me grow and achieve my dreams. Love you.

To my eight beautiful children, thank you for giving me purpose and love every day. To be your father is my greatest joy in life.

Miranda, I love you so much. The life we've created together will forever be our greatest work, and you are the one who truly holds us together.

These old schoolhouse stools bring a vintage touch into a new modern space, making it feel more soulful.

About the Author

LUKE CALDWELL is the star of HGTV's *Boise Boys*
and *Outgrown* and cofounder and owner of the esteemed
design and build firm Timber and Love. *Americana Soul*
is his first book. Luke lives in Boise, Idaho, with his wife,
Miranda, and their eight children.